The Myst
OLMECS

Printed in Mexico

ISBN-13: 978-0-15-352931-3
ISBN-10: 0-15-352931-8

5 6 7 8 9 10   805   11 10 09 08

SCHOOL PUBLISHERS

Visit *The Learning Site!* www.harcourtschool.com

A Discovery in the Jungle

Rumors that giant stone heads had been seen on the Gulf Coast of Mexico had been going around since the mid-1800s. For a long time, no one had paid much attention to them. Then, in 1938, one scientist decided to follow up on the stories. Dr. Matthew W. Stirling went alone into the steamy jungle where heads had been seen. He soon found one. The giant head, carved from a boulder, was $6\frac{1}{2}$ feet tall and weighed 10 tons. The head had a flat nose and thick lips. It was wearing what looked like a cap or helmet.

Stirling returned to Mexico in 1939 to look for more of these strange sculptures. This time, he went with a large expedition. In a place called La Venta, he found four more stone heads and a clay pyramid 100 feet high. Like the first one, the heads all had flat noses and thick lips and were wearing helmets.

Digging deep into the ground, workers also found three pavements made of flat green stones. The stones formed the shapes of jaguars, which are large wildcats.

Dr. Matthew W. Stirling and one of the stone heads he discovered ▶

The Americas' First Civilization?

Scientists knew that great civilizations had existed in Mesoamerica. They had found ruins of pyramids and stone buildings made by the ancient Maya and Aztecs, who had lived in the area centuries ago. But the stone heads were different from anything ever found before. Who had made them?

At the time of the discovery of the stone heads, the oldest known civilization in the region was that of the Maya. Tests done by scientists showed that the monuments at La Venta were more than 3,000 years old. The people who made the stone heads had lived long before the Maya. Scientists began to wonder: Did these people create the first civilization in the Americas?

Olmec ruins ▼

Buried Offerings

The jaguar-shaped pavements Stirling found had been covered with layers of colored clay before they could become weathered. Stirling believed they must have been religious offerings of some sort. Later finds of buried sculptures and more pavements support this theory that the artworks were offerings to the gods.

Who Were the Olmecs?

Scientists called these people the Olmecs. To this day, very little is known about them. They left behind art and artifacts, but many questions remain about the mysterious Olmecs. One thing that scientists know is that in a few hundred years they had turned a simple society of farmers and fishers into a major civilization. But how they did this remains a mystery.

Scientists believe people had migrated into the region by 2000 B.C. They formed small fishing villages. They also raised crops such as maize (corn) and beans. They began to build cities about 3,000 years ago. Olmec culture eventually spread from southern Mexico into Central America. By 1200 B.C., the first great culture in Mesoamerica was thriving.

What's in a Name?

No one knows what the Olmecs called themselves, but in the Aztec language, the name *Olmec* means "rubber people," or "people from the land of rubber." It was the Aztec name for people who lived in Aztec times in what is now southern Mexico. These people made rubber from trees that grow in that hot, wet environment.

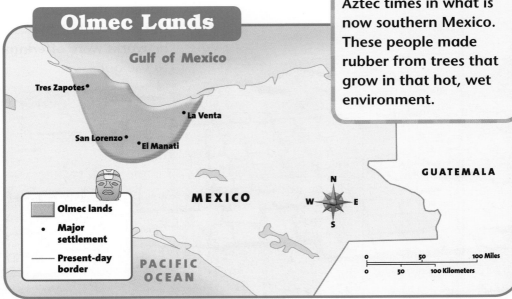

Olmec Lands

Gulf of Mexico

Tres Zapotes

La Venta

San Lorenzo

El Manati

MEXICO

GUATEMALA

Olmec lands

Major settlement

Present-day border

PACIFIC OCEAN

0   50   100 Miles
0   50   100 Kilometers

N
W   E
S

Olmec Centers

The oldest Olmec center discovered so far is San Lorenzo, in southern Mexico. That site had temples and huge stone monuments, including giant heads. It was destroyed about 900 B.C. Its monuments were smashed. What had happened there? One theory is that invaders attacked the city.

La Venta was built later than San Lorenzo. It was an important site between 800 and 400 B.C. North of the city's great pyramid were a number of tombs. Jade sculptures were buried around the city. In one place, workers found 22 standing figures. These sculptures were facing each other in a circle.

After studying these and other Olmec sites, scientists believe that all Olmec centers were built around a raised mound. They believe these mounds were used for religious ceremonies.

About 900 B.C., pyramids began to replace the mounds. Some 200 mounds had houses as well as temples or pyramids on them. A site could be a town as well as a religious center. Later, Olmec cities even had systems of ditches to carry water for crops.

Historians believe these figures are arranged to depict a religious ceremony. ▶

5

A Highly Developed Culture

From the ruins of Olmec centers, scientists have determined that the Olmecs had a social structure that was based on class. At the top were the rulers and the priests. Lower down were crafts-people, farmers, and workers. Proof of this class structure is shown in the different types of housing. There were palaces for the rulers, large homes for the wealthy, and simple huts for the workers.

More proof of the Olmecs' highly developed culture is the fact that they invented a calendar and a system of writing. Symbols carved in stone have survived to show us what Olmec writing was like. However, no one has been able to read the writing.

The Olmecs also had a sophisticated set of religious beliefs. The jaguar was at the heart of Olmec religion. Scientists once thought the Olmecs worshipped just one god—a part-jaguar, part-human figure called a were-jaguar.

Based on their art, the Olmecs seem to have had at least ten other gods. Among these were gods of water, fire, rain, and corn. The Feathered Serpent was an important Olmec god.

The Olmecs may have seen the jaguar as a spirit to be feared and worshipped. ▶

A Sacred Ball Game

A sacred ball game played with a rubber ball is common to all Mesoamerican cultures. The game dates back to Olmec times and was likely their invention. The world's earliest rubber ball was found at an Olmec site. It dates from about 1200 B.C.

The ball court was in the shape of an L. Once the ball was in play, it was not supposed to hit the ground. As in soccer, players did not use their hands. They kept the ball in the air by bouncing it off other body parts.

Historians believe this game was a symbol of a battle between humans (one team) and the gods and spirits (the other team). The rules of the game were perhaps harsh. Historians say that the winning team received gifts, while members of the losing team were sacrificially killed.

In the Olmec ball game, the courts were seen as openings to the underworld. ▼

Art of the Olmecs

The Olmecs produced the earliest art in Mesoamerica. Much of Olmec art differs from that of other cultures in the region, both in the materials used and in style.

In earlier years the Olmecs made art objects out of clay from the region. Then they began trading with people in faraway places. The Olmecs brought home rare materials, such as jade, and began using it for their artwork.

Some Olmec art objects were worn as ornaments. Among these were discs of iron ore that acted as mirrors. The Olmecs pierced holes through them so they could wear them from a cord around the neck. Olmec rulers or priests may have worn the mirrors to make people think they had special powers.

An Olmec mirror ▼

Olmec Science

The Olmecs made advances in science as well as art.

Magnets

Some 2,000 years before Europeans used magnetic needles in compasses, the Olmecs used magnetic stones to determine direction. They even carved statues around natural magnets. An Olmec statue of a sea turtle has a magnet in its snout. The Olmecs may have thought this was how the turtles found their way across the ocean.

Anatomy

The Olmecs also made the earliest known accurate image of the human heart! Experts had thought a book made in 1543 had the first true images of a heart, but a 3,000-year-old Olmec sculpture came first.

The image of the were-jaguar is unique to Olmec art. This creature appears on statues, masks, tiles, headdresses, and axes. The Olmecs also made life-size images of people with the features of crocodiles.

Nearly life-size, hollow, glazed clay sculptures of human infants are also common in Olmec art. Many of these sculptures combine features of both jaguars and infants. These figures are often crying or snarling with open mouths.

Olmec ceramic baby figurine ▶

Those Giant Heads...

The Olmecs are best known for the giant stone heads first found in the jungle. To date, 17 heads have been found. They range from 5 to 11 feet high and weigh up to 20 tons. The heads are made of basalt. This heavy, hard stone is not found in the Olmec region. It had to be brought from as far as 80 miles away. At San Lorenzo the stone was also lifted 150 feet uphill.

The Olmecs did not have beasts of burden, such as horses or oxen. They had not invented the wheel. How did they move the materials for their huge works of art to the sites where they were found? They may have floated the basalt down rivers on rafts. How they got it overland and raised it up to such heights is still a mystery.

Did the Olmecs move their giant sculptures down rivers on rafts? ▼

Yet another mystery is why the Olmecs made these giant heads. One theory is that they are portraits of Olmec rulers. All the heads have head coverings that look like football helmets. These may be the protective helmets that players wore in the sacred ball game. Olmec rulers took part in these games. It is possible that the heads are images of rulers dressed for the game.

A Clue to the Olmecs' Origins?

Some scientists think the faces on the heads look African. This led to a theory that the Olmecs' ancestors came from Africa. However, no proof yet supports the idea of early African settlement of the Americas.

Other scientists think the features on the stone heads look more Asian than African. Most scientists today believe the Olmecs' ancestors crossed into the Americas from Asia during the last Ice Age. This is the main theory about the origin of Native Americans.

Colossal Olmec heads from Mexico

Did Africans Reach the Americas?

According to legend, Abubakari II, a ruler of Mali, wondered what lay across the ocean to the west of Africa. In 1311, he left Mali with a fleet to "find the end of the ocean." He never returned. To some observers, the giant Olmec heads look like people from Mali. They thought the heads might be proof that Abubakari had reached America. We now know that the heads were made 2,000 years before his voyage.

11

Questions That Remain

Around 400 B.C., the Olmec civilization suddenly collapsed. The Olmecs could have been the victims of invaders. Other theories are that their crops failed or trade broke down. Or several events may have combined to bring about the end of the Olmecs. Whatever the cause, the Olmec civilization vanished from the region. Why this happened is one of the many questions that remain about the Olmecs.

Mother Culture of the Americas?

For a long time, scholars thought the Mayan civilization was the first in the Americas. Scientific dating methods eventually showed that the Olmecs had built cities 1,000 years before the Maya did. At a 1942 meeting of experts on the Olmecs, scholars suggested that the Olmec civilization was a mother culture. A mother culture is the culture that first develops certain ideas. These later spread from the source to other surrounding cultures.

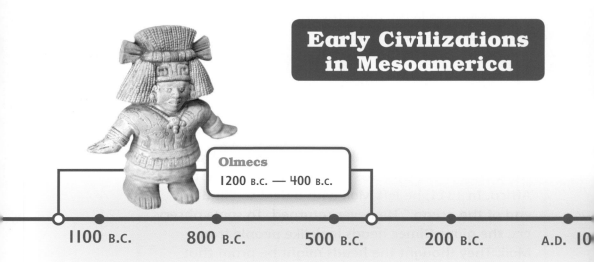

Early Civilizations in Mesoamerica

Olmecs
1200 B.C. — 400 B.C.

1100 B.C.　　　800 B.C.　　　500 B.C.　　　200 B.C.　　　A.D. 10

Peoples in surrounding areas had adopted and imitated Olmec culture and religion. Some experts believe that the Maya based their culture on that of the Olmecs.

New evidence for the Olmecs as a mother culture came out in 2005. A team from George Washington University led by Dr. Jeffrey P. Blomster carried out a long study of Olmec pottery. The team published its findings in 2005. They reported that other ancient cultures had made pottery in the Olmec style. They copied Olmec symbols and designs. However, the team found that only the Olmecs had exported their pottery. The team claimed that these findings support the theory that the Olmecs created and spread their culture.

Some scholars reject this theory. Many still believe the Mayan culture was the mother culture. The Olmec, they say, was one of several "sister cultures." They point out the many ways in which the Olmec and Mayan cultures were alike. This could prove that the two cultures traded ideas.

The debate about whether the Olmec is the mother culture of the Americas is, of course, still going on. Historians will continue to study Olmec ruins and artifacts to try to find answers to many of the questions that remain about these mysterious people.

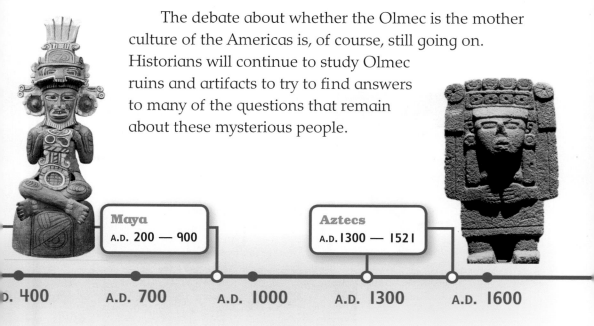

Maya
A.D. 200 — 900

Aztecs
A.D. 1300 — 1521

D. 400   A.D. 700   A.D. 1000   A.D. 1300   A.D. 1600

Old Problems, New Tools

Dr. Richard Diehl of the University of Alabama is another expert trying to find answers about the Olmecs. According to him, a big reason why there are few clues about the Olmecs is that the land in which the Olmecs lived is being damaged. Diehl says that ". . . about 80 percent of the entire Olmec territory . . . has been converted in the past 20 years from jungle to cow pastures and sugar-cane fields." In addition, each year floods bury the land—and any artifacts—under silt. Scientists can no longer find Olmec objects sitting on the ground.

Many Olmec sites still remain covered, waiting to be unearthed. Modern science is helping with this. One scientist, Dr. Sheldon Breiner, uses magnetism to find hidden artifacts. With instruments that detect and measure magnetic fields, he can locate ancient objects deep under the ground. Breiner spent three years mapping San Lorenzo. His magnetic surveys found Olmec artifacts in unsuspected places. At San Lorenzo, he found a giant head that was buried 20 feet underground. Many of the artifacts he has located are still buried. Money to dig them up is not yet available.

Sheldon Breiner discovered this Olmec artifact using a magnetometer. ▼

Another potential source of information about the Olmecs is their writing. Unfortunately, no one has ever been able to read it. Scientists have learned about a language that some desendents of the Olmecs wrote, however, by comparing it to the Mayan language. Perhaps somewhere in the Olmec region is a carving with a message in both Olmec symbols and a known language. Such a carving could hold answers to questions about the mysterious Olmecs.

1 Historians believe the writings on the stone describe events related to the Harvest Mountain Lord, a warrior-king.

2 The warrior-king's name is a combination of two symbols.

3 The Olmecs used bars and dots to indicate numbers. The dot represents the number one and the bar represents the number five. Other numbers are formed by combining dots and bars. These combinations of dots and bars represent dates.

▶ The symbols on a stone carved by descendants of the Olmecs were translated by comparing them with later Mayan symbols.

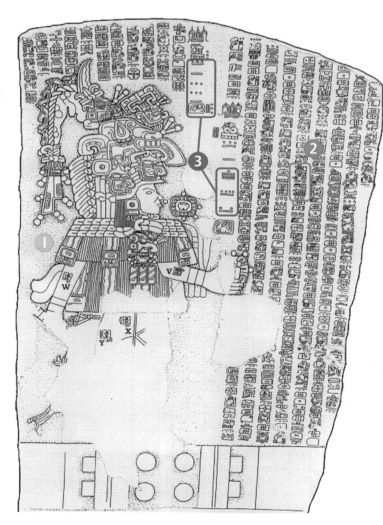

Think and Respond

1. Who were the Olmecs?

2. Why do scientists think the Olmecs carved giant stone heads?

3. What caused Blomster's research team to decide that the Olmec civilization was the mother culture of the Americas?

4. What information do you think could be learned if scientists could read Olmec writing?

5. How is modern science finding answers to questions about the ancient Olmecs?

 # Activity

Which was the mother culture of the Americas—the Olmec or the Maya? Hold a debate. Form two teams. Each team will make a case for one point of view. With your team, prepare an argument supporting your opinions. Take turns presenting arguments and answering points the other team makes. Let the class decide the winner.